A Discovery Biography

ABIGAIL ADAMS

"Dear Partner"

by Helen Stone Peterson
illustrated by Betty Fraser

CHELSEA JUNIORS
A division of Chelsea House Publishers
New York • Philadelphia

For Arthur

The Discovery Biographies have been prepared under the
educational supervision of Mary C. Austin, Ed.D.,
Reading Specialist and Professor of Education, Case
Western Reserve University.

Cover illustration: Janice Fried

First Chelsea House edition 1991

Copyright © MCMXCI by Chelsea House Publishers, a division
of Main Line Book Co. All rights reserved. Printed and bound in
the United States of America.
© MCMLXVII by Helen Stone Peterson

1 3 5 7 9 8 6 4 2

ISBN   0-7910-1402-9

Contents

Abigail Adams: "Dear Partner"

Chapter *1*

A Terrible Night

Eleven-year-old Abigail Smith awoke suddenly. It was before daybreak on November 18, 1755. The bed, shared with her older sister Mary, was shaking. The girls leaped from it and raced down the narrow stairs to the kitchen. The whole house was shaking!

Their mother stood in front of the fireplace, her face white. Their little sister Elizabeth clung to her mother and sobbed wildly. Their father was staring out the window. Abigail watched milk spill over the sides of a bowl on the tottering table.

"What's happening?" she cried.

Suddenly the milk stopped spilling. The house stopped shaking.

Abigail's father turned around. "We have had a terrible earthquake. I'm afraid it has done great harm."

A few minutes later he was hurrying out the door to see how things were in town. He was the minister of the Congregational Church in Weymouth, Massachusetts. He also ran the farm where his family lived.

When he returned, he brought good news. "I don't think that anyone in Weymouth has been hurt. Some chimneys lost a few bricks. That seems to be all."

"What about William?" Mrs. Smith asked anxiously. Abigail's brother William was visiting his uncle in Boston, about twelve miles away.

Mr. Smith nodded. "The danger is greater in the city because of the many brick buildings. I'll ride there at once. And I'll stop at Mount Wollaston."

Grandmother and Grandfather Quincy lived in the big house at Mount Wollaston on the shore road. Abigail spent some of her happiest days with them in their beautiful mansion. The Quincys, her mother's parents, were one of the leading families in Massachusetts.

Massachusetts was an English colony and had an English governor. But the colonists made most of their own laws. Grandfather Quincy had been active in the government a long time. Abigail hated to think that he or Grandmother might have been hurt.

"Come, girls," Mrs. Smith called to them after Father had ridden off on his horse. "It's our duty to do the work we planned."

The girls had planned to make mince pies for Thanksgiving. Their mother was teaching them to cook and sew and spin and weave. "You must know these things so you can manage your own homes some day," she often told them. "Some day you will have your own families."

The girls worked well together. After the dough was mixed, Abigail rolled it lightly into crusts. But her thoughts turned to her father. "Oh, what will he find?"

When her work was done, Abigail slipped into the study and opened a book. She had been sickly as a small child and hadn't gone to school. She studied with her father instead. More than anything, she liked to read.

Abigail was reading when a carriage rolled into their driveway. "My grand-parents have come! So the earthquake didn't hurt them!" Abigail told herself. She ran to greet them.

Grandmother Quincy flung her arms around all three girls. "This is what I said last night:

'I see the moon, the moon sees me
The moon sees three girls I want
to see!' "

Abigail laughed softly.

Grandmother caught sight of the pies. She praised the girls. "Such fine golden crusts! We'll have a good Thanksgiving."

But Abigail wasn't sure. She was still worried.

Her grandparents stayed until Father returned. "William is perfectly all right and so are the others," he reported.

Abigail felt a burst of happiness. Everyone in her family was safe! Now she was sure they would have a good Thanksgiving.

Chapter *2*

Partners for Life

It was a fine winter evening, not long after Abigail's seventeenth birthday. Her older sister Mary was expecting Richard Cranch. Mary was engaged to him.

There was a knock. "Abigail, please let Richard in," called Mary. She was still in front of her mirror and their mother was out.

Abigail opened the door, giving her deepest curtsy. "Welcome, Sir Richard," she said gaily. Then she saw that he wasn't alone. His friend John Adams was with him. Abigail blushed. She wished she had been more proper.

Mary appeared and took Richard into the parlor. Abigail's father invited John into his study. Then he asked Abigail to bring some apples.

Abigail had known John ever since she was a little girl. He lived on a farm in Braintree, four miles away. He had graduated from Harvard College and was getting started as a lawyer.

Abigail returned with a bowl of red apples. On top she had placed a big yellow pear. "It's from a tree that's over 100 years old," she explained.

John looked at Abigail in surprise. Most girls weren't interested in things like that. But he was interested in the fruit trees and everything else on his farm. His friends often called him Farmer John.

John was even more surprised when Abigail left the room, taking with her a book of Shakespeare's plays. Most girls didn't read books like that in their spare time. But John did.

John came back again. Before long he was calling on Abigail often.

Abigail's eyes grew bright with a new happiness. She was falling in love with John. And he was in love with her.

Abigail's mother frowned. She wanted the best for her daughter. John was from a good family, but not a leading

one like the Quincys. Would he ever be anything more than a poor country lawyer? "Please wait," she said when they spoke of marriage.

So Abigail and John became engaged, and waited. Abigail had letters from John when he couldn't make his regular visits to her. "Dear partner of all my joys and sorrows," he wrote.

In time Abigail's mother saw that they knew their own hearts.

Abigail was married to John in 1764, just before her twentieth birthday. Her father read the wedding service. Afterwards there was a wedding feast with grandparents, aunts, uncles, and cousins.

Abigail and John drove off before the feasting had ended. Their farmhouse in Braintree was waiting for them.

Chapter *3*

The Boston Massacre

Abigail hugged her baby. "Now I lay you down to sleep," she whispered as she put her little daughter in the cradle. The baby was named after her but was called Nabby.

Abigail's heart was full of happiness. She and John had been married one year. They had their darling baby. They had their small farmhouse which Abigail loved. John's office was downstairs. His widowed mother lived next door.

Abigail's only worry was America's quarrel with England. Earlier this year England had passed a law ordering the colonies to pay a tax. The Americans were angry. Leaders from the colonies were holding a meeting in New York.

"The tax is unfair because the colonists had no part in making that law," John had told Abigail. "It's our right to make our own laws. We cannot let our rights be taken from us."

John had written down his thoughts about the tax law. Abigail was proud when the newspaper in Boston printed John's words.

Abigail was lifting a golden corncake from the oven when she heard a noise. The next minute John bounded into the kitchen and swept her into his arms.

She saw that he was excited about something important. But he stopped and kissed Nabby's soft cheek gently.

John spilled out his news to Abigail while they ate supper. "I've heard a report about the meeting in New York. The men there agreed that England has no right to tax us without our consent."

"What do you think will happen now?" asked Abigail.

"I think England will remove the tax," John replied.

"Will that end the quarrel between our colonies and England?"

John shook his head. "I don't know."

Early the next year England removed the hated tax. "But we are not giving up our right to make other laws for the colonies," the English rulers declared.

After Abigail read this in the newspaper, she knew the quarrel hadn't ended.

The months flew by. When Nabby was two years old, Abigail and John had their first son. They named him John Quincy after Abigail's grandfather.

Before Johnny had his first birthday the family moved to Boston. John was becoming known as an excellent lawyer. More and more people were also turning to him for advice on government matters. He and Abigail decided his office should be in the city.

By this time England had passed another law ordering the colonies to pay other taxes. Soldiers were sent to Boston to make sure that England's laws were obeyed.

Abigail listened to John's warning.

"These soldiers will surely keep our people stirred up. There is certain to be trouble!"

Sometimes boys threw oyster shells at the soldiers and called them bad names. In the second winter a terrible thing happened. John heard about it and hurried home to tell Abigail.

"The English soldiers have killed three of our men. Others are hurt, perhaps even dying."

Abigail's eyes flooded with tears.

"A mob of young men threw snowballs and chunks of ice at a soldier on duty," John continued. "Other soldiers came running to help him. In the uproar that followed, one of our hotheads tried to grab a gun from a soldier. The soldiers fired."

The next day John had something more to tell Abigail. "I have agreed to be the lawyer for the English Soldiers. No other lawyer would take the case. One said he would help me, however."

"But John!" Abigail gasped, turning pale, "People say the English soldiers murdered our men. They're calling it a massacre."

"The law will decide whether it was murder or self-defense," said John. "In Massachusetts a man has the right to a fair trial. It's my duty to help keep it that way."

"Yes," Abigail nodded. She saw how much courage John had. Some people would accuse him of siding with the English. "I'm proud of you," she said, kissing him.

At their trial the English soldiers were found not guilty of murder. As time passed, all Americans were proud that the soldiers had a fair trial.

And as time passed, Abigail and John watched the quarrel between the colonies and England grow bigger. John moved his family back to the old farmhouse in Braintree where they would be safer. There were two more children now, Charles and Tommy.

The family was together at the farm on April 19, 1775. A horse pounded down the road. Abigail and John heard the rider shout, "The English soldiers are fighting the Americans at Lexington and Concord!"

The Revolutionary War had started.

Chapter *4*

Independence Day

Just two months later, on June 17, Abigail was awakened by the thunder of cannon. "What's happening?" she asked herself.

John wasn't home. He was at the new Continental Congress meeting in

Philadelphia, Pennsylvania. Men from all thirteen colonies were meeting to plan their country's future. They had sent pleas to England, "Let us keep our rights!" They were sending one more plea now.

Abigail dressed quickly. A few minutes later she was at the big fireplace, stirring cornmeal mush for breakfast.

"Where's the battle? Are we winning?" asked five-year-old Charles. Nabby and Johnny and Tommy fixed their eyes on their mother's face.

"I don't know," Abigail answered them steadily.

They were finishing breakfast when a messenger came to the door. "Our men are trying hard to hold Bunker Hill in Charlestown! But the English ships are bombarding them with cannon!"

"Come," Abigail told her oldest son. She and seven-year-old Johnny climbed to the top of their own hill. Looking across Boston Harbor they saw the flash of the thundering cannon.

Later black smoke darkened the sky. "The English are burning the homes and churches of Charlestown!" cried Abigail.

The Americans lost the battle, but they showed how bravely they could fight. Soon General George Washington arrived to lead the soldiers.

Farmers hurried to join his army. Abigail fed them when they stopped at her farmhouse. Women and children fled from Boston to safer places. Abigail fed them too. Food became scarce.

"We can eat huckleberries and milk," Abigail wrote to John.

English soldiers raided towns along the shore, stealing sheep and cows. Would they raid Braintree? Would they set fire to Abigail's home and church?

"We fear them not!" Abigail wrote to John.

It was deadly sickness that struck Braintree next. Abigail got well in time to take care of Tommy who almost died. The maid, who helped Abigail, died. Abigail's mother came to help. She caught the sickness and died too.

Abigail's hand trembled as she wrote to John. "Oh, my bursting heart."

The awful winter passed. In March, 1776, Washington drove the English soldiers away from Massachusetts. Now they would fight the Americans in New York and other places.

"It's time we cut all our ties to England!" Abigail wrote to John. "I long to hear that Congress has declared independence."

Abigail heard from John in July. "A resolution was passed that these united colonies are free and independent states." Abigail felt a rush of joy.

She called to her children. She read aloud the shining words John wrote to her about Independence Day.

"It ought to be solemnized with pomp and parade, with shows, games, sports, guns, bells, bonfires, and illuminations . . . forevermore."

Chapter *5*

"When is Papa Coming Home?"

Abigail had to manage the farm while John was away at the Continental Congress. Farm workers were scarce because the men had joined the army. "I believe I could gather corn and husk it, but I should make a poor figure at digging potatoes," she wrote to John.

Abigail was also her children's teacher.

The schoolmasters marched off to the army saying, "War's begun, school's done." Abigail taught French and Latin to Nabby and Johnny. And she taught Charles and Tommy to read and write.

Whenever she had a spare moment, Abigail sat down to her spinning wheel. No cloth was coming from England. Abigail and her maids must spin and weave home-made cloth. "If we didn't, the children would be naked!" Abigail wrote to John.

The children kept asking, "When is Papa coming home?"

One August day Abigail opened a letter from John. "I'm coming for a visit," he wrote. Smiling, Abigail read the letter to the children. Would Abigail send him a horse to ride home?

"What can I do?" Abigail thought. Their own horse was lame. Good horses were hard to find because the army had taken so many.

Suddenly Charles spoke up. "Mama, I want Papa to come home. Take my dollar and get a horse for Papa."

Abigail kissed her curly-haired boy. "Your father will come. I promise."

Abigail's father sent his horse to John. But John had to put off his visit. Some battles had started around New York City. The Americans were losing them. John was working hard to build a better army. His job was like that of today's Secretary of War.

At last, in October, another message came. Johnny jumped off his pony and ran into the house, carrying the letter.

Several times a week now Johnny swung into his saddle and rode to Boston for the mail.

Abigail read the letter aloud. "I'm starting home," John wrote. Charles and Tommy cheered.

Later they were painting thirteen little stripes on the sleds they would use as soon as snow fell. While they worked, they chanted their favorite verse:

"The English King
    Lost states thirteen!"

How delighted Abigail and all the children were when John reached home. Every day together was a happy one. Then after Christmas John rode away again to Congress.

Another long year dragged by. When John reached home the next winter, Abigail thought he would stay. He had served four years in Congress. He decided not to run for office again right off.

John was home just three weeks when a letter arrived from Congress. The United States wanted France to join the fight against England. Benjamin Franklin was in France, asking for help. Would John go there and work with him?

Tears ran down Abigail's face. Must she and the children lose John so soon again? How long would he stay across the ocean? "We'll be robbed of our happiness," she sobbed.

But she agreed John must go. "It's your duty to our country," she said with courage.

Chapter *6*

Lonely Days, Lonely Nights

"John, I want to take the children and go with you to France," Abigail pleaded.

"With all my heart I wish you could," John replied. "But if an English ship captures me, I'll end up in prison. I may lose my head. I shudder to think what might happen to you and our little ones."

Together Abigail and John made the decision. "No, the family won't go."

But when Johnny pleaded to go, they said yes. It would be good for the ten-year-old boy to spend more time with his father. Johnny could attend school in France. Schools at home were still closed.

Abigail packed trunks for John and Johnny. She sent a barrel of apples to their ship. At the last moment she sent a few chickens. "They will lay fresh eggs for you while you travel," she said.

The family parted on a cold day in February. Month after long month Abigail waited for a letter. The story went around, "The ship was sunk!" Another story went around, "Adams is a prisoner!"

On the last day of June, Abigail had a letter from John. After a dangerous voyage he was safe in Paris. He was working for his country. Johnny was in school.

They came home the next summer. Abigail kissed and hugged them. She thought, "Our family will live together now. I'm so glad."

French ships and French soldiers were fighting on the side of the Americans. John believed that his work in France was done.

But three months later Congress sent him back again. The Americans were winning important battles with the English now. John must be ready to help write the peace treaty when the war was won.

This time John took nine-year-old Charles as well as Johnny. Abigail thought her heart would break. "I cannot swallow my food," she cried.

Again Abigail was the head of the farm and the head of the household. Pretty Nabby helped her mother. Sometimes Abigail took Nabby and Tommy on visits to her two sisters Mary and Elizabeth.

Abigail was brave when she learned that Johnny had gone to Russia. An American diplomat there needed an assistant who could speak and write French. Johnny was only fourteen but he knew the language well.

Without Johnny, Charles grew very homesick. So his father placed him on a ship ready to sail home to Boston.

Unexpectedly the ship stopped in Spain and refused to take the passengers any farther. Abigail lived through anxious months until Charles reached her.

In the fall of 1781 Washington won the last big battle of the war. The United States had won its independence! Abigail was a proud American.

Her thoughts flew to John. "When will my dear partner come home?"

A year later John still wasn't home. He was working on the peace treaty. Lonely Abigail wrote to him. "Only think how the words three, four, and five years' absence sound! They sink into my heart with a weight I cannot express."

Two years later John still had not come home.

The peace treaty was completed, but Congress had asked John to stay in France. He would help write other treaties so that the United States could carry on business with European countries.

"It's my duty to help our new nation grow great and powerful," John wrote. "Yet I cannot live here any longer without you. Will you come?"

Abigail's heart knew the answer. "Yes!"

Chapter *7*

Across Old Ocean

"I'm going to cross Old Ocean! I'm going to join my partner!" That joyful thought kept running through Abigail's mind as she made plans.

"Nabby will go with me," she said. Her daughter was now a very beautiful eighteen-year-old. "Charles and Tommy will stay here."

They would live with their Aunt Elizabeth. Her husband was a minister and teacher. He would prepare the boys for Harvard College.

Abigail's ship, the *Active,* sailed for England on a warm June day in 1784. Abigail was seasick the first afternoon.

"I smell dirt and that makes me sicker!" she groaned. When she was on her feet again, she got the captain to say she could clean the ship. She told the sailors to bring mops and brushes and pails of water mixed with vinegar. Under her watchful eyes they scrubbed the ship from top to bottom.

A few weeks later Abigail and Nabby reached London. But their letter, telling when they would arrive, hadn't reached John. They had to wait for him.

One afternoon a handsome young man came to their hotel. At first glance he seemed a stranger. Then Abigail looked into his eyes. "My son!" she cried. He had been a twelve-year-old boy when she saw him last. Now he was seventeen and quite grown up. No one called him Johnny any longer. He was now John Quincy.

John was in Holland where he had been borrowing money for the United States. He finished his work there and hurried to London.

When he swept Abigail into his arms, all the ache left her heart. The four happy people traveled to Paris. John had rented a mansion outside the city.

Abigail and Nabby went to many gay dinner parties with Benjamin Franklin and Thomas Jefferson. John worked with these men making treaties. John Quincy was his father's secretary.

"I see plays and operas in Paris and I like them," Abigail wrote to her sisters. "But my heart keeps returning to my own home."

She loved to get letters from Charles and Tommy. Elizabeth wrote, "Your boys are doing well in their studies. And at dancing school the misses all like to have Charles for a partner."

In the spring Congress appointed John to be the first American Ambassador to England. John Quincy decided to return home and enter Harvard.

"Some day our country will need you for a leader," Abigail said. "Study hard so you will be ready."

A few days later Abigail was packing for the move to London. John entered the room, laughing. "I hear that seven traveling companions were waiting for John Quincy on the ship."

"Who?" asked Abigail quickly.

"Dogs! General Lafayette sent seven dogs to George Washington. John Quincy is to see that they get good food and fresh water."

Abigail laughed so hard that she couldn't pack anything for a few minutes.

Chapter *8*

The Ambassador's Lady

"King George may not be friendly to you," people warned Abigail and John. "Remember, he didn't like to lose America!"

Abigail thought about that warning now. She was at the palace, waiting to meet the King. John had been presented already in a private meeting.

"Oh, I don't tremble before kings," Abigail told herself.

She and Nabby and 200 other guests stood in a circle around a large room. Abigail looked elegant. She wore a long white gown over a wide hoop.

Abigail saw the King enter. He was short and red-faced. Smiling and bowing, he stopped to talk with each person. He did these same things when he reached Abigail.

But he did something more that came as a big surprise. The King kissed Abigail's left cheek!

A few days later Abigail and John and Nabby moved from their hotel to a large house on Grosvenor Square. Abigail had to hire a butler, cook, coachman, upstairs and downstairs maids.

"Will Congress send enough money for all these expenses?" Abigail worried.

Soon she saw that she could save money by doing her own shopping.

The newspapers poked fun at her: "Farmer's wife, going to market!"

The newspapers poked fun at John: "Penny pincher! He doesn't give dinner parties an ambassador should give."

The fact was that Congress didn't send enough money. Abigail and John weren't rich. John could have earned plenty of money as a lawyer. But he had given that up long ago when his country needed him.

"We'll act our part well," Abigail said. They would meet the costs somehow. Notes were sent, inviting all the foreign ambassadors to come for dinner.

"What shall I feed them?" Abigail asked herself.

Before she made up her mind, a wonderful thing happened. A fishing boat arrived from Boston. The captain gave John a giant codfish caught off New England. Abigail's eyes twinkled. "We'll have American food! The codfish will be perfect, served with a tasty sauce." Her dinner party was a success.

At the end of the first year in England, Nabby was married to handsome Colonel William Smith. He was the secretary in the American Embassy. At the end of another year Abigail was a happy grandmother. "My charmer," she called Nabby's little boy William.

At the end of the third year John finished his term as Ambassador. Abigail was eager to see her sons. She wanted to go home.

One day, during their last summer in England, John took Abigail to the seashore. She saw men and women bathing in the ocean. They didn't do that back home.

"I'll try it!" said Abigail. She went into a bathhouse. An attendant helped her pull on socks and a flannel gown and an oilcloth cap. Abigail stepped into the salt water.

"It's delightful!" she told John. "We should have our own bathing beach at Braintree!"

Chapter *9*

The Vice-President's Lady

Abigail and John's three handsome sons welcomed them home.

"My dear boys!" Abigail cried.

John Quincy was now studying law. He had finished Harvard with high honors. Charles and Tommy were still students there.

Home for Abigail and John was no longer the small farmhouse. They had bought a large house in nearby Quincy.

Abigail was busy placing the furniture in their new home. John bought cows. After that he bought sheep and pigs and oxen.

"Your father turned into Farmer John fast!" Abigail wrote to her daughter. Nabby and her family were living near New York City.

In the spring, John was elected the first Vice-President of the United States. It was a great honor. George Washington was elected the first President. The capital was then New York City. Abigail couldn't go there with John when the new government started.

"I must do something with all the animals!" she said. She sold as many as she could. She found someone to take care of the others.

On a June day Abigail reached the comfortable house John had rented in New York. The next morning she visited Martha Washington. The two ladies became warm friends.

Abigail gave pleasant dinner parties for the members of Congress and their wives. She also held open house one evening a week. Everyone was welcome.

John talked with Abigail about the things the new government was planning. She listened carefully. Often she told him what she thought.

"No one is more interested in political subjects than I," Abigail wrote to her sister Elizabeth.

The next year the government moved to Philadelphia. During her second year there, Abigail had a long, serious illness.

When she could stand the bumpy ride in the carriage, John took her home. She got back her health. But she didn't try to live in Philadelphia again while John was Vice-President. Each year when Congress finished work, John hurried home to Abigail.

One spring day Abigail received a message that made her proud. President Washington had appointed John Quincy to the position of Minister to Holland. He was only twenty-six years old. Yet he was already an ambassador, as his father had been. Tommy would be John Quincy's secretary.

"It's one of my chief blessings to have sons worthy of the trust of our country," Abigail wrote to her boys. "Serve it with honor as your father does."

Chapter *10*

First Lady

"I'll be with my partner tonight," Abigail told herself as her carriage rattled along.

It was a May morning in 1797. John was now the second President of the United States. Abigail hadn't been with him when he took office in March. She was looking after his sick mother who was at the end of her long life. After the funeral Abigail left for Philadelphia.

Suddenly Abigail's carriage jerked to a stop. Abigail saw that another carriage had drawn close. A gentleman stepped quickly out.

"John!" cried Abigail.

"I had to come meet you," John said. "I can't get along without you one more day!" Abigail finished her journey in the President's carriage and at the President's side.

A few days later the new First Lady held a reception. After that she began to give official dinner parties. She also spent much time calling on the ladies who visited her.

"I must return each visit," Abigail wrote to her sister Mary. "I get up at five o'clock in the morning. That's the only way I can do all my work."

Abigail also paid attention to everything that happened in the government. "Politics are as natural to me as breathing," she once remarked. So it was natural that John talked with her about the quarrel between the United States and France.

The quarrel grew until soon the two nations were on the brink of war. Many Americans wanted to fight. They belonged to the party that had voted for John. They were angry when John sent men to France to make peace.

"I know I will not be chosen President a second time," John told Abigail.

"You did right," Abigail answered him. Years later all Americans agreed. The young country was saved from a war that would have hurt it.

During John's third year as President, Tommy was back with his parents. Abigail was delighted. Tommy opened a law office in Philadelphia. John Quincy was now Minister to Prussia, which was a part of Germany.

One evening Abigail gave a dinner party for Tommy and twenty-eight of his friends. The girls looked lovely in their best dresses. While dessert was being served, Tommy spoke quietly to his mother. "Do you have any objection to our dancing this evening?"

"None in the world," Abigail answered. So the young people danced until midnight. The rooms rang with their laughter.

When Congress finished work that spring, Abigail started home ahead of

John. On her way she stopped in New York City to see Charles. She did so with a heart heavy with sorrow over this beloved son.

Charles was a lawyer. He had a wife whom Abigail liked and two pretty little girls. But other things hadn't gone well for Charles. When he lost money John Quincy had placed in his care, it was more than Charles could bear. He was drinking heavily. At the age of twenty-nine, Charles was a sick and broken man.

Alone in her room, Abigail wept. She thought back through the years. She could almost hear the little boy say, "I want Papa to come home. Take my dollar and get a horse for Papa."

Six months later Charles died.

Chapter *11*

The President's House

"We're lost!" said Abigail.

The road was nothing more than two tracks through a thick forest. Abigail's coachman walked ahead and broke off branches so the carriage could squeeze by the trees. Finally a woodcutter directed them to the road for Washington.

It was November 1800. Abigail was on her way to join John in the new capital.

Four-year-old Susan, Charles' older daughter, was with her.

When she reached the city, Abigail saw the houses were set far apart. Ugly stumps were left where trees had been chopped down. "This is still a wilderness city," thought Abigail.

She caught her first glimpse of the new President's House, later called the White House. It looked twice as big as her church at home. "This House is built for the ages to come," she wrote in a letter to her sister Mary.

Abigail found that not a single room in the President's House was finished completely. There was also no place outdoors to dry the washing. So she told the servants to hang the wash in a long parlor, later called the East Room.

She also told the servants, "Please keep all the fires going." The rooms felt cold and damp.

John was delighted to have Abigail and Susan with him. Soon, however, the little girl became sick. Abigail was awakened by dreadful sounds from Susan's room. She was gasping for breath.

"Get a doctor!" cried Abigail. A servant ran for one who lived nearby. The doctor boiled vinegar in a kettle. He had Susan breathe in the steam. In the morning she was better.

In December the votes for President were counted. John was not elected for a second term. He would not be President after March third.

"You have been a nation-builder. You kept the peace," Abigail said loyally.

"I hope future Presidents do as much for our country as you have."

She lifted her head proudly. "I will do my duty while we are here." She gave dinner parties and receptions in the unfinished President's House. Her guests included members of Congress, judges, and heads of many departments. Abigail invited their wives too.

In the middle of February Abigail and Susan started home. John would follow in March. As she rode out of Washington, Abigail thought about the future.

"We'll spend the rest of our lives in Quincy, my partner and I. He will have the farm and his books. Our children and grandchildren will visit us." Abigail laughed aloud and gave Susan a hug.

"The family will find me in the dairy early in the morning. I'll be skimming the cream from the milk so I can make good butter for all of us."

And that's what happened. Abigail and John enjoyed many more years together in Quincy. They felt great happiness when John Quincy was made Secretary of State. "I pride myself on being the mother of such a son," Abigail said.

Abigail was dead when her son John Quincy was elected the sixth President of the United States. John knew how proud she would have been. Tears rolled down his old cheeks as he thought about her.

"*Dear partner* of all my joys and sorrows . . ."